BIBLICAL PERSPECTIVES

A GUIDE TO THE TRUE GRACE OF GOD

VOL I

BY THOMAS FRANCIS FISCHER

WITH AHAVA SARAH FISCHER

Published by:

BIBLICAL
PERSPECTIVES
PUBLISHING

(Scripture quotations are from the King James version of the Bible.)

Cover Design, Book Synopsis & Editing by Ahava Sarah Fischer.

ISBN:0991177908
ISBN-13: 978-0-9911779-0-5

DEDICATION

I dedicate this book to my Lord and Savior Jesus Christ.
Thank you Lord for saving me. Thank you Lord for loving me. Thank you
Lord for teaching me. Thank you Lord for giving me your Holy Spirit. I
love you Lord. I also thank my beautiful, God-fearing wife Ahava who has
been such an incredible blessing to me. You are my gift from God. I love
you honey. You're amazing.

CONTENTS

BIBLICAL PERSPECTIVES

ACKNOWLEDGMENTS

I thank my mom for being a remarkable mother who exemplifies unconditional love. I thank my brothers and sisters-in-law, nieces and nephews for being committed to family. And I thank all my brothers and sisters in the Lord who have been an encouragement to me and for helping me in my walk with the Lord.

1Peter 5:12,

" By Silvanus, a faithful brother unto you, as I suppose,

I have written briefly, exhorting, and testifying that this is the

True Grace of God wherein ye stand ."

PREFACE

My name is Tom Fischer.

I am 49 years old. I have been a born-again Christian for over 22 years and have been studying the Holy Bible consistently during this passage of time.

In 2008, I had a supernatural experience with the Holy Spirit and angels.

Angels grabbed my hands, poured what felt like hot, molten, putty into each palm. It was the baptism by fire.

Immediately afterwards I started getting people healed in the name of Jesus.

When people get healed supernaturally, it is from the grace of God.

Simply put, the gospel of Jesus Christ is the Gospel of Grace and I am a grace preacher. The impetus for the writing of this book comes from seeing the definition of grace being corrupted.

Actually, this has been happening for a long time.

I call this corruption "false grace". It is also called, "narrow grace", "hyper grace", "greasy grace", "sloppy agape", "easy believism" amongst other names. I call it false grace because there is a true definition of grace.

1 Peter 5:12 , says, "By Silvanus, a faithful brother unto you, as I suppose, I have written briefly, exhorting, and testifying that this is the true grace of God wherein ye stand".

The false grace that is being taught by many, including some well-known, popular preachers is very dangerous for a number of reasons. The main reason I see is that it turns believers into "do nothings".

It causes Christians to think "resting in the Lord" means doing nothing, so as to not be found guilty of trying to be justified by works.

Resting in the Lord does not mean, "do nothing". It means, stop trying to be justified in the eyes of God by your own works, or by the keeping of the law.

We are, however, called to do good works, which we will do if we truly are obedient sons of God.

Ephesians 2:10 says, "For we are his workmanship, created in Christ Jesus unto good works, which God hath before ordained that we should walk in them."

Having the right perspective of God's word is the key to understanding what grace truly means and we come to this perspective by looking at the preponderance of scripture, meaning, all of scripture.

I don't need to eliminate any scripture in order to make my doctrine work.

I have a reverent fear of God and I do not pick and choose what to keep as well as what to eliminate from the bible.

In this book, I will look at individual scriptures and share with you what I believe is an accurate biblical perspective according to the true grace of God.

I am a True Grace preacher.

Chapter 1

Genesis 4:7

Genesis 4:7 says, "If thou doest well, shalt thou not be accepted? and if thou doest not well, sin lieth at the door. And unto thee shall be his desire, and thou shalt rule over him."

There are many who think that we, as believers in God, cannot overcome sin and that is why Jesus gave his life for us. Is that true? Did Jesus give his life because we could not overcome or did he give his life to pay the penalty for sin?

Jesus died to pay the penalty for sin.

Everyone, after reaching a certain age knows that it's wrong to commit murder. Those who keep on murdering are those who have consistently hardened their hearts towards the command not to murder. Jesus did not pay the penalty for someone to keep murdering.

When Jesus paid the penalty for sin, he didn't eliminate sin. Sin still exists and people commit sin everyday. The price he paid was for everyone, but not everyone wants the gift.

If Cain had no ability to overcome, why would God tell him he must master sin long before Jesus paid the penalty for sin?

Cain did have the power to overcome by simply asking God to help him.

However, he didn't want God; which is tantamount to not wanting Jesus.

Chapter 2

Genesis 6:5-8

Genesis 6:5-8 says, "And God saw that the wickedness of man was great in the earth, and that every imagination of the thoughts of his heart was only evil continually.

And it repented the Lord that he had made man on the earth, and it grieved him at his heart.

And the Lord said, I will destroy man whom I have created from the face of the earth; both man, and beast, and the creeping thing, and the fowls of the air; for it repenteth me that I have made them.

But Noah found grace in the eyes of the Lord."

Why would Noah find grace in the eyes of the

Lord?

Hasn't God always been gracious?

Does God's grace allow man to go on in wickedness?

Noah found grace in the eyes of the Lord because he was a righteous man. He didn't allow himself to be corrupted by the wickedness around him. Note also that Noah had to build an ark. God didn't just throw down a fully-built ark for Noah and his family to walk into.

He had much to do to prepare for his deliverance, as the book of James says, "faith without works is dead."

Chapter 3

Genesis 13:7-13

Genesis 13:7-13 says, "And there was a strife between the herdmen of Abram's cattle and the herdmen of Lot's cattle: and the Canaanite and Perizzite dwelled then in the Land. And Abram said unto Lot, Let there be no strife, I pray thee, and between my herdmen and thy herdmen; for we are brethren. Is not the whole land before thee?

Separate thyself, I pray thee, from me: if thou wilt take the left hand, then I will go to the right; or if thou depart to the right hand, then I will go to the left.

And Lot lifted up his eyes, and beheld all the plain of the Jordan, that it was well watered every where, before the Lord destroyed Sodom and Gomorrah, even as the garden of the Lord, like the land of Egypt, as thou comest unto Zoar.

Then Lot chose him all the plain of Jordan; and Lot journeyed east: and they separated themselves the one from the other. Abram dwelled in the land of Canaan, and Lot dwelled in the cities of the plain, and pitched his tent toward Sodom.

But the men of Sodom were wicked and sinners before the Lord exceedingly."

2 Peter 2 describes Lot as a righteous man. But Lot, being a righteous man was still drawn by the flesh as he desired Sodom and he almost lost his life because of it. Two angels had to literally manifest themselves in the natural and bring Lot and his family out before the place was destroyed.

The bible speaks of the destruction of Sodom and Gomorrah as examples of those who experience eternal judgment. So, despite the fact that Lot was a righteous man, he was exposing himself to judgment because of lust. And he almost perished because of it.

Chapter 4

1Kings 22:19-22

1Kings 22:19-22 says, "And he said, Hear thou therefore the word of the Lord: I saw the Lord sitting on His throne and all the host of heaven standing by Him on His right hand and on His left.

And the Lord said, Who shall persuade Ahab, that he may go up and fall at Ramoth Gilead? And one said on this manner and another said on that manner.

And there came forth a spirit and stood before the Lord and said, I will persuade him.

And the Lord said unto him, Wherewith?

And he said, I will go forth and I will be a lying spirit in the mouths of all his prophets.

And he said, Thou shalt persuade him and prevail also: go forth and do so."

Demons multitask.

One demon can affect many people at the same time.

This demon found about 400 men who were in agreement with it and so it was easy for it to oppress them all simultaneously.

Note also that just because the Lord sent it, doesn't mean it was what God wanted. God had already laid down the law concerning what is the right way to behave. King Ahab was simply reaping what he had sown.

He was wicked.

God was merely facilitating what was happening because of man's decisions.

God is love, but He gives man free will.

Chapter 5

1Chronicles 4:9-10

1Chronicles 4:9-10 says, "And Jabez was more honourable than his brethren: and his mother called his name Jabez saying, Because I bare him with sorrow.

And Jabez called on the God of Israel, saying, Oh that thou wouldest bless me indeed, and enlarge my coast, and that thine hand might be with me, and that thou wouldest keep me from evil, that it may not grieve me!

And God granted him that which he requested".

I heard a well-known preacher say the following.

I quote, "But God says this, Jabez was more honorable and the only reason given is that he prayed this prayer. He looked to God instead of looking to men".

What is wrong with that statement?

This statement is saying that Jabez praying the prayer is what made him more honorable than his brothers. It claims that this is the reason God granted his request. Is that accurate?

Is it not accurate to say that God answered his prayer because he was an honorable man, more so than others? The Scripture says that he was more honorable than his brothers. That is why his prayer was answered.

This well-known preacher has to look at this scripture in this way in order for his doctrine to continue to work. His analysis of this scripture causes Christians to think that the honorable thing here is merely to pray to God for a blessing and has nothing to do with Jabez actually being more honorable than his brothers.

Chapter 6

2Chronicles 34:25

2Chronicles 34:25 says, "Because they have forsaken me and have burned incense unto other gods, that they might provoke me to anger with all the works of their hands; therefore my wrath shall be poured out upon this place and shall not be quenched".

The Jewish people were not only trying to be justified by works, they were also practicing evil behavior.

They were turning to idol worship.

This is the evil that God called, "the work of their hands". The work of their hands was not their keeping of the sacrificial system. Their sin was not the sacrificial system.

The Old Covenant Jews were capable of turning from sin by getting God's word in them.

When the bible speaks of turning from sin it is not saying that you will never sin again. Rather, it teaches turning away from "practicing" sin.

Psalm 119:11 says, "Thy word have I hid in mine heart, that I might not sin against thee".

Those who hid his word in their hearts turned away from the wicked "works" of their hands. They turned away from "practicing" sin.

The same is true today. By getting Jesus (the word) in us, we turn away from "practicing" sin.

Chapter 7

Psalm 25:14

Psalm 25:14 says, "The secret of the Lord is for those who fear Him and He will make them know His covenant."

I believe the word covenant is being used here to describe the everlasting covenant of grace and not the covenant of law, even though this scripture is from the Old Testament.

God looks at those who fear Him, meaning those who obey the commands He has put on everyone's heart and then He makes sure they know about Jesus.

There are many Christians that teach inaccurately that God doesn't look at a person's heart before revealing Jesus Christ.

It's true that God loves everyone and wants everyone to believe in His Son Jesus, but it is clear to see in life that the wicked don't understand love.

Those who go on in their own willful ways deceiving and being deceived, just don't get it.

A man needs to humble himself in order to see the glory of the Lord.

God opposes the proud, but gives grace to the humble. Jesus is that grace.

Chapter 8

Psalm 40:7

Psalm 40:7 says, "Then said I, Lo, I come in the volume of book it is written of me."

One of the worst things being taught today is the discouragement of reading the bible.

Those who deter believers from studying holy scripture, assert that the bible is not the word of God, while emphasizing that Jesus is the word of God.

Yes, Jesus is the word of God, but it is senseless to say the bible is not the word of God.

It seems to me that some are teaching this because they need to eliminate so much of scripture to make their doctrine work. What better way to make wrong doctrine acceptable than to discredit the bible?

The word of God is every word that comes out of the mouth of God. This being the case, we recognize Holy Scripture as the word of God.

"Man does not live on bread alone, but on every word that proceeds out of the mouth of God. "- Matthew 4:4.

We learn about Jesus by studying the bible. In fact, we need to know all of what Jesus said before and after the cross, including the letters and epistles which are inspired by the Holy Spirit.

Jesus said in John 16:12-13, "I have yet many things to say unto you, but ye cannot hear them now. Howbeit when he, the Spirit of truth, is come, he will guide you into all truth: for he shall not speak of himself; but whatsoever he shall hear, that shall he speak: and he will show you things to come."

These two verses by Jesus tell me that everything written by Paul, Peter, John, James, Jude and the writer of Hebrews (if not written by Paul) were the very words of Jesus.

These men were chosen by God and led by the Spirit of God to write the word of God, which is God.

Chapter 9

Psalm 78:13-22

Psalm 78:13-22 says, He divided the sea and caused them to pass through and He made the waters stand up like a heap. Then He led them with the cloud by day and all the night with a light of fire.

He split the rocks in the wilderness and gave them abundant drink like the ocean depths.

He brought forth streams also from the rock and caused waters to run down like rivers.

Yet they still continued to sin against Him, to rebel against the most high in the desert.

And in their heart they put God to the test by asking food according to their desire.

Then they spoke against God; They said, "Can God prepare a table in the wilderness?

Behold, He struck the rock so that waters gushed out and streams were overflowing; Can He give bread also?

Will He provide meat for his people?"

Therefore the Lord heard and was full of wrath; and a fire was kindled against Jacob and anger also mounted against Israel, because they did not believe in God and did not trust in His salvation."

In this portion of scripture we see that engaging in sin is comparable to not believing or not trusting in God's salvation.

God even considered it evil of the people to ask for something that was a desire of their flesh.

They wanted meat.

They weren't satisfied with the provision that God had for them.

Many Christians today don't recognize this same

thinking in their own lives. They don't consider sin to be an issue. They get upset when they don't get what they want. This is common among those who follow an unbalanced prosperity gospel.

God does want to prosper us, but many Christians today (because of certain well-known preachers) believe in the prosperity of God through a corrupted perspective.

They think they deserve to have everything they want according to their will. They set their hearts on the blessing instead of the one who blesses.

It's amazing how these ancient people of Israel saw all these staggering signs from God and still turned away from him. Yet Christians do the same thing today. (A gift or sign from God is often forgotten or taken for granted.)

The Old Testament relates these events for our benefit so that we will refrain from doing the same evil things that they did.

Chapter 10

Psalm 119:11

Psalm 119:11 says, "Thy word have I hid in mine heart, that I might not sin against Thee".

Those who hid His word in their hearts turned away from the wicked "works" of their hands. They turned away from "practicing" sin. The same is true today. By getting Jesus (the word) in us, we turn away from "practicing" sin.

Those who teach that sin is not an issue anymore are teaching erroneously.

The issue with Christians is not about stumbling in sin. The issue is about willfully "practicing" sin or committing sin over and over without responding to the convicting power of the Holy Spirit.

This Christian life is a Spirit-led life.

If we are led by the Spirit we will not "practice" sin because we will be sensitive to the Spirit telling us if we sin.

If you begin to lose your peace, there is a good chance you are beginning to practice sin.

Do not harden your heart.

Respond to His correction by repenting and your peace will return.

Chapter 11

Isaiah 1:19

Isaiah 1:19 says, "If ye be willing and obedient, ye shall eat the good of the land".

Some of today's grace preachers say that believing this verse as a new covenant believer is no different than having an old covenant mindset.

An old covenant mindset means, stop trying to be justified by law. It doesn't mean to do as you please and forget about His commands.

God wants to bless us, but we are the ones who need to put ourselves in a position of receiving. This is done through obedience and a willingness to submit to God and what He tells us to do, in order to receive his promises.

Matthew 7:8 says, For everyone that asketh receiveth: and he that seeketh findeth: and to him that knocketh it shall be opened.

God doesn't just drop things on our lap.

If a believer is receiving a lot of blessings from God, I can assure you he or she is "doing" a lot of right things in the eyes of God.

Being obedient means that you are going to obey what the Lord tells you to do. That obedience will put you in a position to receive from God.

Chapter 12

Isaiah 26:3

Isaiah 26:3 says, "Thou will keep him in perfect peace, whose mind is stayed on thee: because he trusteth in thee".

So, the one who is trusting in the Lord is the one whose mind is consistently on the Lord. If you lack peace, it's because your mind is not stayed on the Lord. I know some will not like this because tragedies happen in life that rob peace for a short or long period of time.

This statement is not meant to be lacking in compassion.

It's simply an observation from the word of God. Inaccurate teaching on grace would say you have perfect peace when you are born-again and that you simply need to believe that.

This is true, but it leaves out responsibility on our part to keep our minds stayed on him. This scripture shows that there is a responsibility on our part. Those who teach grace inaccurately are very much set against a believer thinking they have any responsibility in spiritual matters.

I believe that there are many believers who are living in defeat because they are not diligent in keeping their minds stayed on the Lord.

They have one foot in the world and one foot in God and that simply doesn't work.

It's a recipe for misery.

Chapter 13

Jonah 3:10

Jonah 3:10 says, "And God saw their works, that they turned from their evil way, and God repented of the evil, that He said He would do unto them; and He did it not".

There are several things that I want to discuss concerning this portion of scripture. When reading the word of God, perspective is everything.

First, this verse says that God repented of the evil that He was going to do. In the New Testament we learn that God does no evil and that God is love. I think it is important to realize that people living before the cross could face judgment at any time because of sin.

God is a just judge.

Satan, the accuser, would accuse and God, the judge, would decide if he, Satan, was accurate in his accusation based on law because the people lived under law. The devil doesn't tell God what to do.

Nevertheless, we see in Jonah 3:10 that God is gracious and merciful even before the cross because He turns from judgment based on repentance. The good works that the people of Nineveh started doing was considered repentance in the eyes of God.

James 2:26 says faith without works is dead. God saw the repentance, or works of the people and stopped judgment. God has always been gracious and He responds to repentance.

In the New Testament Jesus preached repentance and told the disciples to preach repentance. Changing one's mind always results in a change of behavior. If you say you trust in Jesus and your behavior hasn't changed, you haven't changed your mind.

Chapter 14

Zephaniah 1:18

Zephaniah 1:18 says, "Neither their silver nor their gold shall be able to deliver them in the day of the Lord's wrath; but the whole land shall be devoured by the fire of His jealousy: for He shall make even a speedy riddance of all them that dwell in the land".

Some teach that the wrath of God was satisfied by Christ and His work on the cross.

To be accurate, the wrath of God was satisfied by the work of Christ on the cross for those who believe and not for those who refuse to believe.

The wrath of God still remains on everyone else. The "day" of the Lord is still yet to come, where God pours out His wrath on those who do not accept Jesus as King.

John 3:36 says. "He that believeth on the Son hath everlasting life: and he that believeth not the Son shall not see life; but the wrath of God abideth on him".

I think a lot of people who have misunderstood grace tend to think that because Jesus took the sins of the whole world, it means God's wrath is totally satisfied.

Jesus has taken the sins of the whole world, but that gift still has to be received by faith and that is done through repentance.

Some will argue against repentance by saying, for example, the thief on the cross whom Jesus said would be with Him in paradise, didn't have time to show true repentance. That man repented by acknowledging that he was wrong.

He humbled himself.

Repentance doesn't necessarily mean you now have to do penance to prove it. John the Baptist said to bear fruits in keeping with repentance.

The man on the cross next to Jesus did bear fruit.

He showed love towards Jesus by publicly acknowledging that Jesus was innocent.

Chapter 15

Matthew 3:8

Matthew 3:8 says, "Bring forth therefore fruits meet for repentance".

There are some teaching that repentance is not needed. Some are teaching that all you have to do is believe that Jesus took the sins of the whole world and that is considered repentance.

Mark 1:15 says, "And saying, the time is fulfilled, and the kingdom of God is at hand: repent ye, and believe the gospel."

This scripture shows two things to do. Repent AND Believe the gospel.

Repentance means more than just, "stop trying to be justified by the keeping of the law".

It also means, "turn from sin". If someone who claims to believe in Jesus continues to sin, they will not produce fruit showing that they have repented. When a person repents, there is evidence. Fruit will be produced.

Matthew 7:19-20 says, "Every tree that bringeth not forth good fruit is hewn down, and cast into the fire. Wherefore by their fruits ye shall know them."

Some are teaching that repentance is needed, but only once, when you receive Christ as your Lord and Savior. This thinking gives people a license to sin because they become convinced that they have done no wrong when they sin.

Anybody who thinks this way, also tends to downplay sin in the lives of those who need to come to Christ as they themselves don't consider sin to be an issue.

The fact that Jesus took the sins of the whole world doesn't mean that sin doesn't exist. Rather, it means that you are no longer being condemned for your sins when you repent and believe the gospel.

Chapter 16

Matthew 6:14

Matthew 6:14-15 says, "For if ye forgive men their trespasses, your heavenly Father will also forgive you: But if ye forgive not men their trespasses, neither will your Father forgive your trespasses".

Some say that Jesus is teaching law in these passages. They say that your sins are forgiven even if you fail to forgive. This is a wrong perspective. Jesus was not teaching law.

Jesus is the grace of God.

He came to teach grace.

Forgiving everyone is gracious. When you do so, you are acting like Jesus. Jesus forgave you of your sins and so you do the same.

1John 2:6 says, "He that saith he abideth in Him ought himself also so to walk, even as He walked."

Looking back at Matthew 6:12, it says, "And forgive us our debts, as we forgive our debtors."

This is like a trade off.

Our sins are forgiven, AS we forgive others.

To think that I can expect the forgiveness of my sins, while failing to extend forgiveness to others is the height of hypocrisy.

Chapter 17

Matthew 6:22

Matthew 6:22 says, "The light of the body is the eye; if therefore thine eye be single, thy whole body shall be full of light".

This means that when you are totally focused on who Jesus is and what he teaches, your whole body is full of light.

Some say, "No, your whole body is full of light because of you accepting Jesus' work on the cross and being born-again as a result."

I have met countless professing Christians whose eyes show little light because they are not submitting to the whole word of God. Being in strife and having anger and resentment towards others fills you with darkness.

Even committed Christians let darkness into themselves from time to time by what they look at and take in, such as, unholy movies, books and magazines. The amount of light in you is based on the amount of light you let in.

Do you want a lot of light or do you want darkness?

It is your choice.

God does not force you to receive anything.

Chapter 18

Matthew 7:21

Matthew 7:21 says, "Not everyone that saith unto me, Lord, Lord, shall enter into the kingdom of heaven; but he that doeth the will of my Father which is in heaven".

Inaccurate teaching on grace clings to the doctrine of once saved, always saved (OSAS).

As believers in Jesus we are called sons and daughters of God. I don't ever cease to be my heavenly Father's son, because I believe in Jesus. But, does this really solidify the doctrine of OSAS? What do the scriptures say?

I will point out 3 places in scripture that make the point that sonship does not automatically imply obedience, or eternal security.

Matthew 21:28-31 says, "But what think ye? A certain man had two sons; and he came to the first, and said, Son, go work to day in my vineyard. He answered and said, I will not: but afterwards he repented and went. And he came to the second, and said likewise. And he answered and said, I go, sir: and went not. Whether of them twain did the will of his father"?

2Corinthians 6:17 says, "Wherefore come out from among them and be ye separate, saith the Lord, and touch not the unclean thing: and I will receive you, and I will be a Father unto you, and ye shall be my sons and daughters, saith the Lord Almighty".

The point here is the condition - How are you received? Touch not the unclean thing and then you are received.

This is not saying, get right first and then He receives you.

It means that once you have come to a recognition of the truth and have repented, then live up to that truth.

Luke 15:24 says, "For this my son was dead, and is alive again; he was lost, and is found...".

This scripture is connected to the story of the prodigal son. The son chose to leave his father's household. He didn't cease to be a son, but on his return to his senses (repentance), his father made the statement found in verse 24, he " was DEAD, and is alive again; he was LOST, and is found".

Chapter 19

Matthew 8:28-33

Matthew 8:28-33 says, "And why take ye thought for raiment? Consider the lilies of the field, how they grow; they toil not, neither do they spin:

And yet I say unto you, that even Solomon in all his glory was not arrayed like one of these.

Wherefore, if God so clothe the grass of the field, which today is, and tomorrow cast into the oven, shall he not much more clothe you, O ye of little faith?

Therefore take no thought, saying, what shall we eat? or, What shall we drink? or, Wherewithal shall we be clothed?

(For after all these things do the Gentiles seek:) for your heavenly Father knoweth that ye have need of all these things.

But seek ye first the kingdom of God, and His righteousness: and all these things shall be added unto you".

Some say these verses make it clear that you can have all you need without doing anything.

But, do these verses really make that point?

Take note, how these things, food, water, clothes, are not added to you, UNTIL you seek first His kingdom AND His righteousness.

If I am wrong about this, why are so many people dying daily of starvation? It is certainly not God's will for this to happen. What does it mean to seek his kingdom and his righteousness?

Throughout the gospels we see Jesus using parables to explain what the kingdom of heaven is like. Read the gospels and take note of when Jesus is speaking of the kingdom.

You don't have to work for it, but you do have to line up your thinking with the kingdom. You have to come into agreement with kingdom principles. An example of a kingdom principle is forgiving. You must forgive. It is not an option.

There is no strife in the kingdom.

There is no anger in the kingdom.

There is no lust in the kingdom.

There is no stealing in the kingdom.

There is no deception in the kingdom.

You have to learn how the kingdom operates.

Along with this, you have to seek his righteousness, which is Jesus Christ. Not your own righteousness.

Living in anger and strife and lust or anything else that is contrary to the way Jesus lived, is the same as living according to your own righteousness.

When you seek Jesus, you are submitting to Him so that He can form His character in you because you must walk as He walked.

Chapter 20

Matthew 10:7-15

Matthew 10:7-15 says, "And as ye go, preach, saying, The kingdom of heaven is at hand. Heal the sick, cleanse the lepers, raise the dead, cast out devils: freely ye have received, freely give.

Provide neither gold, nor silver, nor brass in your purses, Nor scrip for your journey, neither two coats, neither shoes, nor yet slaves: for the workman is worthy of his meat.

And into whatsoever city or town ye shall enter, enquire who in it is worthy; and there abide till ye go thence. And when ye come into an house, salute it.

And if the house be worthy, let your peace come upon it: but if it be not worthy, let your peace return to you.

And whosoever shall not receive you, nor hear your words, when ye depart out of that house or city, shake *off the dust of your feet.*

Verily I say unto you, It shall be more tolerable for the land of Sodom and Gomorrah in the day of judgment, than for that city."

Take notice of what they were to preach:

"The kingdom of heaven is at hand".

Jesus didn't say, "I have come to teach law to Jews living under law." Jesus is the grace of God and He taught the people about the kingdom of heaven.

Yet, we see here that cities and towns are rejected by Jesus for not accepting His message.

Peace is given to those who are worthy.

What does it mean to be worthy?

Well, the apostles stayed with people who received their message.

As they went about their business of proclaiming the message, they were to shake the dust off their feet against those who rejected them.

Some would say, "Just keep loving on them and they will come around eventually. Don't cause any problems or get people upset."

I'm not against continually loving on people, but we don't see Jesus wasting time.

People need to repent.

Shaking the dust off your shoes would be considered unloving and arrogant by many today, but it is what Jesus instructed them to do.

Chapter 21

Matthew 10:38

Matthew 10:38 says, "And he that taketh not his cross, and followeth after me, is not worthy of me".

What does it mean to follow Jesus?

Well, Jesus was constantly doing good. He was preaching against evil. Jesus was constantly working.

John 5:17 says, "But Jesus answered them, My Father worketh hitherto, and I work".

Working does not automatically imply that you are doing it on your own strength. If someone believes in Jesus they will eventually act like Jesus, which means that they will be working for Him. They will be led to act and speak by the Holy Spirit.

And if someone is working hard for the Lord it doesn't mean that person is trying to be justified by works. It means that Jesus lives in Him and it has become apparent to all.

Chapter 22

Matthew 12:36

Matthew 12:36-37 says, " But I say unto you, That every idle word that men shall speak, they shall give account thereof in the day of judgment.

For by thy words thou shalt be justified, and by thy words thou shalt be condemned."

According to some, once you're in Christ after having trusted in His finished work on the cross, there can't possibly be idle words that can condemn you.

In this verse of Scripture, Jesus is teaching on repentance as He did everywhere he went.

Receiving the true grace of God means repenting.

Repenting doesn't just mean stop trying to be justified by the keeping of the law. It also means turning from sin, such as speaking idle words. Even idle words can condemn a person to hell.

These scriptures indicate how there is no such thing as once saved, always saved.

What if you get born-again and grow in the Lord and than many years later turn from the truth and begin practicing idle words coming out of your mouth? Will your righteousness save you? No, your own righteousness will never save you.

It is only His righteousness that saves you. and He does not speak idle words.

"He that saith he abideth in Him ought himself also so to walk, even as He walked". -1John 2:6.

This doesn't mean if you speak idle words you are going to hell. This is why repentance matters. If you speak idle words, you repent and His shed blood cleanses you from all unrighteousness.

The person who practices speaking idle words without repenting is the person who is beginning to trust in his own righteousness.

That very person will be condemned for speaking idle words because that person is trusting in his own righteousness.

Matthew 12:36-37 says, "every idle word...". If idle words can't condemn a person after trusting in the finished work of the cross, why would Jesus say "every idle word..."?

That's like saying that none of the words you speak after trusting in the finished work of the cross can possibly be idle words.

I've had to repent of plenty of idle words after trusting in Jesus. The reason my heart did not become hard from speaking idle words is because of the act of repentance.

If I didn't see the need to repent, I may have continued and begun to "practice" this sin, thereby starting to turn away from the Lord and trusting in my own righteousness.

Chapter 23

Matthew 18:15-16

Matthew 18:15-16 says, "Moreover if thy brother shall trespass against thee, go and tell him his fault between thee and him alone: if he shall hear thee, thou hast gained thy brother.

But if he will not hear thee, then take with thee one or two more, that in the mouth of two or three witnesses every word may be established".

Some say that Jesus was teaching Jews how to live by the law. They say that this scenario does not apply to New Covenant believers who believe in the finished work of the cross.

However, look at what Jesus goes on to say in verse 17.

"And if he shall neglect to hear them, tell it unto the church: but if he neglect to hear the church, let him be unto thee as an heathen man and a publican".

If this portion of scripture is relating to Jews living by the law, why bring the church into this matter?

Jesus taught Jews what the law really means and how to live by grace. Those who reject Jesus' definition of grace are themselves rejected, according to Jesus' own teaching.

Jesus taught grace.

Chapter 24
Matthew 25:34-36

Matthew 25:34-36 says, "Then shall the king say to them on His right hand, Come, ye blessed of my Father, inherit the kingdom prepared for you from the foundation of the world:

For I was an hungred and ye gave me meat: I was thirsty, and ye gave me drink: I was a stranger, and ye took me in: Naked, and ye clothed me: I was sick, and ye visited me: I was in prison, and ye came unto me".

This is not a "do-nothing" gospel.

A person shows evidence of believing by what he does. Some say quoting scripture like this promotes a "works" gospel, or that it exhibits trying to be justified by works.

That is not the case.

There are the "works" of God that he prepared for us and there is a striving to be justified by works.

Romans 2:10 says: "But glory, honor, and peace, to every man that worketh good, to the Jew first, and also to the Gentile."

People who understand true grace realize that glory, honor and peace comes to anyone who worketh good because Jesus is faithful to bring it about.

There are those who, not yet believing in Jesus, will receive glory, honor and peace by working good and eventually come to believe when they see the grace coming to them.

This is because the love of God is intended to lead a man to repentance. God knows who belongs to Him, even if they haven't come to believe in Jesus yet.

Chapter 25

Luke 12:33

Luke 12:33 says, "Sell that ye have, and give alms; provide yourselves bags which wax not old, a treasure in the heavens that faileth not, where no thief approacheth, neither moth corrupteth".

Some are constantly preaching about taking all there is to take and milking dry every drop of blessing from the Lord.

The emphasis seems to be on receiving unmerited favour, that is interpreted as basking in worldly treasures.

It is obvious that the Lord wants to bless us, but we don't have to pursue these blessings as if it is our obligation to get as much as possible.

Jesus taught more about giving and being a servant, but this teaching is not popular with many Christians.

Some preach getting rich so emphatically that I get the sense that they are simply feeling guilty for being so wealthy.

In my observation, these preachers desperately want some of their followers to be rich as well so that they can justify their excessive lifestyles.

Jesus emphasized giving more than receiving.

Chapter 26

John 11:25-26

John 11:25-26 says, "Jesus said unto her, I am the resurrection, and the life: he that believeth in Me, though he were dead, yet shall he live: And whosoever liveth and believeth in Me shall never die. Believe thou this"?

Some teaching actually tries to make people believe that the body they are in now can live eternally without ever dying in the natural.

This puts a meaning on scripture that is not there. Not one person documented scripturally has ever been able to pull this off, but now all of a sudden we have believers who think this is possible because of the way they interpret scripture.

Elijah and Enoch did not "pull" this off.

They were taken by God.

They are the only two ever to ascend in this manner and that is not enough to form a doctrine since multiple millions have died in the natural.

Hebrews 9:27 says, "And it is appointed unto men once to die, but after this the judgment:...".

The natural body has to die a natural death in order for the believer to be clothed with the everlasting body. Something new does not come to life until the old dies.

1Corinthians 15:42-44 says, "So also is the resurrection of the dead. It is sown in corruption; it is raised in incorruption: It is sown in dishonor; it is raised in glory: it is sown in weakness; it is raised in power: It is sown a natural body; it is raised a spiritual body. There is a natural body, and there is a spiritual body".

Some people choose to place a meaning on the finished work of the cross that God never put there.

Chapter 27

John 15:1-6

John 15:1-6 says, "I am the true vine, and my Father is the husbandman. Every branch in me that beareth not fruit He taketh away: and every branch that beareth fruit, He purgeth it, that it may bring forth more fruit. Now ye are clean through the word which I have spoken unto you. Abide in me, and I in you.

As the branch cannot bear fruit of itself, except it abide in the vine; no more can ye, except ye abide in me. I am the vine, ye are the branches:

He that abideth in me, and I in him, the same bringeth forth much fruit: for without me ye can do nothing. If a man abide not in me, he is cast forth as a branch, and is withered: and men gather them, and cast them into the fire, and they are burned".

This portion of scripture as well as others show clearly that there is no such thing as, "once saved, always saved".

Some teachers take away accountability and responsibility. This could put believers in the position of being a branch that is thrown into the fire for not producing fruit. Some say there is no effort to produce fruit.

They use the argument that a fruit tree is not trying to produce it's own fruit. But that is not a good comparison. The fruit of the Spirit is not produced without your cooperation. This comparison with a fruit tree works if a person remains in Christ, but the issue that is presented in Scripture is that it is possible to be "out of Christ."

The issue that I am presenting is that it is possible to lose your salvation after believing and being found, "in Him". Some have argued that this is focusing on the negative, or attempting to bring fear to people.

Since when is preaching all of the word of God bringing fear or focusing on the negative?

Chapter 28

John 15:16

John 15:16 says, "Ye have not chosen me, but I have chosen you, and ordained you, that ye should go and bring forth fruit, and that your fruit should remain: that whatsoever ye shall ask of the Father in my name, He will give it to you".

Some love this verse because they think they can easily justify wanting anything.

Many who think this way fall into the trap of wanting to get rich. At some point they end up losing a lot and also causing others loss. Greed takes over and they chase after the blessing instead of the one who blesses.

When reading scripture, you must look at the

preponderance of scripture, rather than taking one scripture and making a doctrine out of it. As an example, we can look at other scriptures pertaining to receiving whatever we ask for.

1John 5:14-15 says, "And this is the confidence we have in Him, that, if we ask any thing according to His will, He heareth us: And if we know He hear us, whatsoever we ask, we know that we have the petitions that we desired of Him".

The key words here are, "according to His will".

The Lord knows what He has for you. You shouldn't compare yourself to others and what they have. God has many blessings for you and He holds you responsible for what He has given you.

Matthew 13:12 says, "For whosoever hath, to him shall be given, and he shall have more abundance: but whosoever hath not, from him shall be taken away even that he hath".

We have a responsibility and the Lord holds us accountable for everything that we receive.

We need to know who we are and what we really

want without becoming greedy. God expects us to produce fruit according to what is given to us.

Look at what Matthew 21:43 says about this: "Therefore I say unto you, The kingdom of God shall be taken from you, and given to a nation bringing forth the fruits thereof".

The kingdom of heaven is wealthy. If it is taken from you, you will be made poor.

Again, in 1Corinthians 4:2 it says, "Moreover it is required in stewards, that a man be found faithful".

You will find that as you are consistently faithful to God in all ways, your desires will line up with what He has planned for you.

This could mean having your daily needs being met with no lack, or receiving supplies of millions of dollars because he wants you helping greater numbers who need financial help.

Chapter 29

John 19:30

John 19:30 says, "When Jesus therefore had received the vinegar, He said, It is finished: and He bowed His head, and gave up the Ghost."

Some have put a definition on "It is finished", that God never placed there. When Jesus said, "It is finished", he wasn't saying "Do nothing".

He was saying, "I have now made the way clear for you to come to God freely for salvation, by grace through faith."

Contrary to 'doing nothing' , we are required to do the works we were made to do.

Jesus said in Matthew 7:21, "Not everyone who says

to me, 'Lord, Lord, will enter the kingdom of heaven, but only the one who DOES the will of my Father who is in heaven."

When Jesus said, "It is finished", He wasn't saying that He had no further instructions.

Look at what Jesus said to the disciples in John 16:12-13: "I have yet many things to say unto you, but ye cannot bear them now. Howbeit when he, the Spirit of truth, is come, he will guide you into all truth".

This means that the words written by Paul, Peter, John, James, Jude and Hebrews (if not written by Paul) are the words of Jesus. The letters and epistles are the word of God and are meant to keep believers on track so they don't fall away from the truth.

Chapter 30

Acts 8:22-23

Acts 8:22-23 says, "Repent therefore of this thy wickedness, and pray God, if perhaps the thought of thine heart may be forgiven thee. For I perceive that thou art in the gall of bitterness, and in the bond of iniquity".

This was Peter's response to Simon, who wanted to pay the apostles for the power to impart the Holy Spirit through the laying on of hands. It's a very strong rebuke from an apostle to a new believer.

True grace confronts evil and doesn't just sweep it under the rug.

Here's an example of how some modern day believers would have responded to Simon: "Simon my brother, you are so much better than that. You don't need to buy the gift of God. God will give it to you freely. Just receive brother and remember how big the cross is."

Those who would have responded that way would have corrected Peter's harsh manner. However, Peter holds a high level of honor in the eyes of God and was privileged to write Holy Scripture.

His approach serves to teach us, rather than requiring our correction.

What's also notable about this situation with Simon is that he was a brand new believer. Usually there is much leniency with new believers and yet Peter responded the way that he did.

Chapter 31

Romans 1:18

Romans 1:18 says, "For the wrath of God is revealed from heaven against all ungodliness and unrighteousness of men, who hold the truth in unrighteousness;".

Some teachers try to convince their audience that the wrath of God has been satisfied for everyone.

Is this true?

This is true for those who are in Christ and not for unbelievers. These teachers attempt to make you believe that because the sins of the whole world have been taken by Jesus, God no longer considers anyone an enemy.

Some teachers will use scripture such as

2Corinthians 5:19 - "To wit, that God was in Christ, reconciling the world unto Himself, not imputing their trespasses unto them; and hath committed unto us the word of reconciliation".

But, these teachers fail to acknowledge the next verse, which reads, "Now then we are ambassadors for Christ, as though God did beseech you by us: we pray you in Christ's stead, be ye reconciled to God".

The last part of verse 20, which reads 'be ye reconciled to God' means to repent.

Let's go back to Romans 1:18 that I quoted at the beginning of this paragraph. The last part of the verse says, "...who hold the truth in unrighteousness".

The right perspective is the key to rightly dividing the word of God.

The words, "...who hold the truth in unrighteousness" refers to those who know the truth but continue in their own willful ways.

Persisting in old ways demonstrates not truly

trusting in the righteousness of the Lord, but in their own righteousness.

There will be many who think they are right with God, who actually are not.

Colossians 3:5-6 says, "Mortify therefore your members which are upon the earth; fornication, uncleanness, inordinate affection, evil concupiscence, and covetousness, which is idolatry: For which things' sake the wrath of God cometh on the children of disobedience:"

If the wrath of God is satisfied for everyone, why is this wrath still coming?

Chapter 32

Romans 1:28

Romans 1:28 says, "And even as they did not like to retain God in their knowledge, God gave them over to a reprobate mind, to do those things which are not convenient;"

This portion of scripture clearly states that men know the truth because God has put it into the hearts of everyone. Romans 1:20 says that men are without excuse.

As men lust after the flesh while ignoring the obvious commands of God, God himself gives them over to more and more of this vileness, so that they come to the point of not even realizing they are wrong.

I am a grace preacher, but grace is no license to sin.

Grace enables us to turn from sin. There is teaching in the body of Christ that lets people off the hook for sin.

Wrong teaching doesn't confront sin. It teaches things like, "God believes in you even if you don't believe in God". This is true, but it is a subtle way of not confronting sin.

Jesus and the apostles preached that men should repent. Preaching repentance does not mean you are condemning others. It doesn't even mean that you are being judgmental or hypocritical (unless you are practicing the very same things).

Don't preach that people should turn from lust if you are lusting. For hypocrites are condemned. While preachers of mercy are rewarded. Preach mercy, but warn people in love, because God is just. He will not go against His word.

His word clearly states that people will go to hell forever for not turning away from sin.

Chapter 33

Romans 3:31

Romans 3:31 says, "Do we then make void the law through faith? God forbid: yea, we establish the law".

The law was fulfilled, not abolished.

Jesus fulfilled the law because the law had to be fulfilled. The sacrificial system only *covered* the sins of the people, it did not remove it.

Hebrews 10:4 says, "For it is not possible that the blood of bulls and of goats should take away sins".

There is teaching in the body of Christ that tends to make people feel as if they are trying to be justified by law if they are doing good works. No Christian doing good works is coupling those works with a sacrificial system of blood from bulls and goats.

The Jews weren't sprinkled with blood because of good works. They were sprinkled with blood to cover sins committed in ignorance. Trying to be justified by the keeping of the law was not synonymous with doing good works as some teachers would have you believe.

Granted, it is true that there are religious people who do try to be justified by works. However, these teachers have Christians so terrified of being accused by God of trying to be justified by works, that they do nothing, and think that this is 'resting'.

Resting in the finished work of the cross does not mean, do nothing.

Chapter 34

1Corinthians 4:6

1Corinthians 4:6 says, "And these things brethren, I have in a figure transferred to myself and to Apollos for your sakes: that ye might learn in us not to think of men above that which is written, that no one of you be puffed up for one against another".

Wrong teaching on grace comes mainly from well-known ministers. That's how it spreads quickly. They are great orators and often good-looking and well-packaged. Their ministries are large and prosperous.

Many Christians flock to their teaching and defend it as gospel, but Paul is saying here that those who do this are going beyond what is written.

Those who follow these teachers cast aside many scriptures that refute this wrong teaching, and they simply ignore the scriptures that they don't like.

They use talking points.

I can quote a hard scripture refuting this false grace teaching and many times the response will be, "there is no condemnation in Christ" or "It is finished".

Summing up these points briefly, totally takes those words out of context in order to apply them to the doctrine they have come to embrace.

Jesus said in Matthew 4:4, "It is written, Man shall not live by bread alone, but every word that proceedeth out of the mouth of God".

If a certain scripture doesn't fit into the doctrine you have come to embrace, then you have not balanced the word in your life.

Jesus said in John 14:26, "But the comforter, which is the Holy Ghost, whom the Father will send in my name, He shall teach you all things, and bring all things to your remembrance, whatsoever I have said unto you".

When I hear someone teaching on grace, I observe if they are continually using the same scriptures over and over without quoting scriptures that hold the believer accountable. Then, I begin to hear scripture from the Holy Ghost that shows how wrong an unbalanced message on grace can be.

True grace does not need to eliminate any scripture.

Chapter 35

1Corinthians 9:16

1Corinthians 9:16 says, "For though I preach the gospel, I have nothing to glory of: for necessity is laid upon me; yea, woe is upon me, if I preach not the gospel".

Paul, who understood that we are not justified by works, still held the belief that he "had" to preach the gospel.

Matthew 7:21 says, "Not everyone that saith unto me, Lord, Lord, shall enter into the kingdom of heaven; but he that doeth the will of my Father which is in heaven".

It was God's will for Paul to preach the gospel.

Acts 9:15-16 says, concerning Paul, "But the Lord said unto him, Go thy way: for he is a chosen vessel unto me, to bear my name before the Gentiles, and kings, and the children of Israel: For I will shew him how great things he must suffer for my name's sake".

There is a teaching in the body of Christ that tries to convince Christians that they don't have to do anything. Christians that believe this teaching will slowly come to the point of not being able to hear the Lord because they don't believe there are instructions for them to do anything.

We are called to serve, just as Jesus came to serve.

Chapter 36

2Corinthians 8:15

2Corinthians 8:15 says, "As it is written, He that had gathered much had nothing over; and he that had gathered little had no lack".

In this portion of scripture Paul is speaking of the churches in Macedonia about the gift of money that they promised to give to those in need. Those believers were financially poor, yet rich in many other ways.

Paul made the point that living as a believer is not about making ourselves rich. It's about helping others in need and recognizing that we have no lack as believers because God is our source.

There is an overemphasis in the body of Christ about getting rich in this world's wealth. I'm not against being abundant with money. In fact, I welcome it, but it's not something that we need to pursue.

Chase after the one who blesses and the blessings will chase you down. Those who get led astray by inaccurate teaching on grace become greedy and self-absorbed.

God has continually given me what I need without even asking for it. He has given me the desires of my heart that have been there for years without having to continually pester Him for them.

Jeremiah 29:11 says, "For I know the thoughts I think toward you, saith the LORD, thoughts of peace, and not of evil, to give you an expected end".

Many translations will say, "...plans to prosper you...". I believe the KJV translation, which I use throughout this book, is also saying that, but a modern perception of the language could make it a bit difficult to understand this.

"An expected end", would be a prosperous end, or life. The plans are His and not ours.

Wrong teaching on grace tends to move away from the truth that we are not our own. As believers we belong to Him and have been bought at a price.

He owns everything and gives to those He wants to give to.

Chapter 37

Galatians 2:16

Galatians 2:16 says, "Knowing that a man is not justified by the works of the law, but by the faith of Jesus Christ, even we have believed in Jesus Christ, that we might be justified by the faith of Christ and not by the works of the law: for by the works of the law shall no flesh be justified".

Focusing on the four words in this scripture that read, "works of the law", inaccurate grace teaching will leave out the words, "of the law" and latch on to one word - 'works'.

By doing so, those good works done by faith are lumped together with the works done while trying to be justified by the law.

Those who tried to be justified by the keeping of the law were insisting on people being circumcised in the flesh.

This thinking causes those who are doing good works to think they are trying to be justified by their good works. This breeds believers who are afraid to do the works of the Lord for fear of being condemned for trying to be justified by works.

The works of the law means trying to keep the law on your own strength. It has nothing to do with goods deeds done in the humility that comes from faith.

Chapter 38

Ephesians 2:8-10

Ephesians 2:8-10 says, "For by grace are ye saved through faith; and that not of yourselves: it is the gift of God: Not of works, lest any man should boast. For we are His workmanship, created in Christ Jesus unto good works, which God hath before ordained that we should walk in them".

There is a difference between trying to be justified by works and that of doing the good works which God has prepared for us to do. As discussed, the inaccurate teaching on grace tends to group all works into one category; trying to be justified by works.

Inaccurate grace teachings will quote verses 8 and 9, but leave off verse 10. Usually when the word of

God is referring to those who are trying to be justified by works, it is referring to those who are following the sacrificial system of justification.

It seems that those who have an inaccurate understanding of grace have fear in them concerning works. It seems they fear that if they do good works it may be that they are inadvertently trying to be justified by them and so they avoid good works so as to not be accused of trying to be justified by works.

This is unhealthy fear as opposed to a reverent fear of God.

Chapter 39

2Timothy 2:17-19

2Timothy 2:17-19 says, "And their word will eat as doth a canker: of whom is Hymenaeus and Philetus; Who concerning the truth have erred, saying that the resurrection is past already; and overthrow the faith of some.

Nevertheless the foundation of God standeth sure, having this seal, The Lord knoweth them that are His. And, let every one that nameth the name of Christ depart from iniquity".

Some teach that the resurrection has already occurred.

This Preterist view is embraced by some because it enables them to dismiss correction found throughout the letters and epistles. In fact, those who embrace a full Preterist view believe that the resurrection occurred in AD70 and so nothing written in the bible after the cross applies to Christians today.

This teaching allows for charismatic speakers to sway the gullible with many lies and they get away with it even as 2Timothy 4:3 says, "For the time will come when they will not endure sound doctrine; but after their own lusts shall they heap to themselves teachers, having itching ears;".

The Preterist view is so easily debunked. If this view were accurate, the dead would have come out of their graves and we know that hasn't happened because there are plenty of dead bodies still in tombs prior to and after AD70.

Also, we have not seen the return of Jesus Christ in the manner that He left. Acts 1:11 says, "Which also said, Ye men of Galilee, why stand ye gazing up into heaven? This same Jesus, which is taken up from you into heaven, shall so come in like manner as ye have seen him go into heaven".

Chapter 40

James 2:20

James 2:20 says, "But wilt thou know, O vain man, that faith without works is dead?"

A believer will do the works of the Lord because that is what true faith produces.

This is not saying God is a slave driver. It is saying that true faith will, without a doubt create a believer who not only does good works, but is eager to do good works.

Inaccurate teaching on grace insists that you need not do anything. This thinking causes people to purposely do nothing to prove that they are "resting" in the Lord.

Resting in the Lord does not mean do nothing.

It means, stop trying to be justified by your own works.

Grace truly received produces a believer eager and emboldened to do good works.

Chapter 41

James 5:19-20

James 5:19-20 says, "Brethren, if any of you do err from the truth, and one convert him; Let him know, that he which converteth the sinner from the error of his way shall save a soul from death, and shall hide a multitude of sins".

Wrong teaching on grace doesn't believe that sin can separate a believer from God.

It's important for believers to recognize that the letters and epistles were written as letters of correction to the churches.

In this portion of scripture, James is addressing the brethren. He is not addressing the lost world. The lost people of the world at that time were not in the churches hearing the letter written by James. He is addressing believers. The early church teachers were diligent to keep the congregation in line with truth.

Straying away from truth was a serious matter, unlike today's sloppy teaching of grace that doesn't confront any wrong doing. It is possible to confront wrong behavior without condemning people.

There is way too much teaching on grace that says correction is not needed, but yet we see correction everywhere in scripture.

It seems the writers of scripture thought it necessary to address sin in the body of Christ.

Chapter 42

2John 1:7

2John 1:7 says, "I say this because many deceivers, who do not acknowledge Jesus Christ as coming in the flesh, have gone out into the world. Any such person is the deceiver and the antichrist."

I believe this scripture could apply to those who follow "Christ Consciousness" teaching.

This is a New Age teaching that uses the teaching of Jesus, but without Jesus.

Love without Jesus.

Victory without Jesus.

Healing without Jesus and so on.

This wicked teaching makes Jesus out to be just another messenger of a universal message and that

Jesus Christ is not God nor the only way to God.

But God, in His faithfulness has made sure this scripture is found in the bible because He foresaw the wickedness of Satan and his scheming.

Chapter 43

Revelation 3:1-5

Revelation 3:1-5 says, "And unto the angel of the church in Sardis write; These things saith He that hath the seven Spirits of God, and the seven stars;

I know thy works, that thou hast a name that thou livest, and art dead.

Be watchful, and strengthen the things which remain, that are ready to die: for I have not found thy works perfect before God.

Remember therefore how thou hast received and heard, and hold fast, and repent.

If therefore thou shalt not watch, I will come on thee as a thief, and thou shalt not know what hour I will come upon thee.

Thou hast a few names even in Sardis which have not defiled their garments; and they shall walk with me in *white; for they are worthy.*

He that overcometh, the same shall be clothed in white raiment; and I will not blot out his name out of the book of life, but I will confess his name before my Father, and before his angels".

False grace teaching says that nothing you do can cause you to lose your salvation. My name has not been written in the book of life because I got born-again.

My name was already in the book of life. Names are not added to the book, they are blotted out at the end of a person's life if they don't believe that Jesus is Lord.

This is because God is the God of the living and not the dead. He made everyone to live. People chose to reject His one and only way of salvation.

Keep in mind that these are the words of Jesus after His finished work on the cross.

If you will do a word search with the word "works", you will notice how Jesus refers to a believer's works when addressing all the churches in Revelation 2 and 3 and it is not to commend the believer.

False grace teaching simply will not address these scriptures found in the book of Revelation.

Enough said ... for now.

ABOUT THE AUTHOR

Thomas Fischer is a global evangelist and minister.
His media-based street healing ministry documents supernatural miracles
that occur in everyday events as led by the Holy Spirit. His ministry is
followed on YouTube by a worldwide audience. Thomas and his wife
Ahava Fischer actively do the works of the Great Commission.
They also disciple believers and teach the Pure Gospel.

www.thomasfrancisfischer.com
www.biblicalperspectivestv.com
http://www.youtube.com/mrtomff7
http://tomff7.blogspot.com/
www.facebook.com/biblical.perspectives
www.facebook.com/BiblicalPerspectivesTrueGrace

5331091R00063

Printed in Great Britain
by Amazon.co.uk, Ltd.,
Marston Gate.